Kitchen Science

Science Experiments

THAT

FIZZ

AND

BUBBLE

FUN PROJECTS FOR CURIOUS KIDS

by Jodi Wheeler-Toppen

CAPSTONE PRESS
a capstone imprint

Edge Books are published by Capstone Press,
151 Good Counsel Drive, P.O. Box 669, Mankato, Minnesota 56002.
www.capstonepub.com

Books published by Capstone Press are manufactured with paper
containing at least 10 percent post-consumer waste.

Library of Congress Cataloging-in-Publication Data
Wheeler-Toppen, Jodi.
 Science Experiments that fizz and bubble : fun projects for curious kids / Jodi
Wheeler-Toppen.
    p. cm.—(Edge books. Kitchen science)
 Summary: "Provides step-by-step instructions for science projects using
household materials and explains the science behind the experiments"—Provided
by publisher.
 Includes bibliographical references and index.
 ISBN 978-1-4296-5425-8 (library binding)
 ISBN 978-1-4296-6251-2 (paperback)
 1. Gases—Experiments—Juvenile literature. 2. Bubbles—Experiments—Juvenile
literature. 3. Science—Experiments—Juvenile literature. I. Title. II. Series.

QC161.2.W45 2011
507.8—dc22

Editorial Credits
Lori Shores, editor; Veronica Correia, designer; Sarah Schuette, photo stylist;
    Marcy Morin, studio scheduler; Wanda Winch, media researcher;
    Eric Manske, production specialist

Photo Credits
All photos by Capstone Studio/Karon Dubke

Printed in the United States of America in Stevens Point, Wisconsin.
062011   006228WZVMI

TABLE OF CONTENTS

Introduction

SIZZLING SODA 4

Bubble Juice 6

Double Bubbles 8

Fizzle Out 10

Personal Puffer 12

Bobbing Blobs 14

Foaming Fountain 16

Not Quite the Midas Touch 18

Fire Away! 20

Inflation Station 22

Soda Shooter 24

Glossary 26

Read More 30

Internet Sites 31

Index 31

.... 32

Introduction

Most people picture scientists in laboratories surrounded by bubbling test tubes. But you don't have to be a scientist to have your own lab right in your kitchen, complete with bubbles.

You can do loads of experiments using things from around your house. Grab a straw and blow into a glass of water. The air goes into the cup where it is surrounded by liquid. Presto! You have a bubble—a **gas** that's surrounded by a liquid.

gas—a substance that spreads to fill any space that holds it

Sometimes when you mix ingredients together, they combine to create something new. This process is called a **chemical reaction**. When bubbles show up, you know the new thing is a gas.

You'll have a fizzing good time with these experiments. Are you ready? It's time to get popping!

chemical reaction—a process in which one substance changes into another

SIZZLING SODA

Usually you shouldn't taste your experiments. But here's an exception. Add a little pizzazz to your orange juice, and turn it into orange soda!

What you need:

- 2 cups orange juice
- large glass
- ¼ teaspoon (1.2 mL) baking soda
- spoon

HY·TOP
ALL NATURAL
Baking Soda
Hundreds of Household Uses
NET WT. 16 OZ (1 LB) 454g

If you use more baking soda, the drink will fizz wildly. But it will also taste bitter!

1 Pour orange juice into a large glass.

2 Add baking soda.

3 Stir the juice to start the fizzing.

Why it works:

Orange juice contains citric **acid**. Mixing baking soda and an acid creates **carbon dioxide**. Carbon dioxide is the same gas that is used to make sodas bubbly. It's also the gas that makes you burp after you drink them!

acid—a substance with a sour taste that reacts easily with other substances
carbon dioxide—a colorless, odorless gas made of oxygen and carbon

Bubble Juice

Soap bubbles are made of a gas that's surrounded by a thin layer of liquid. The liquid is strong enough to hold in air, but light enough to float. This corn syrup in this bubble solution makes the bubbles super strong.

What you need:

- 1 cup (240 mL) warm water
- bowl
- 2 tablespoons (30 mL) corn syrup
- 2 tablespoons (30 mL) liquid dish soap
- spoon
- pipe cleaner

What you do:

1 Pour water into a bowl.

2 Add corn syrup and liquid dish soap.

3 Stir gently with a spoon until the corn syrup is completely mixed into the water and soap.

4 Twist the end of a pipe cleaner into a loop. Dip the loop into the bubble juice.

Put on a long-sleeved cotton shirt and see if you can bounce the bubbles on your arm.

5 Blow gently through the loop to make bubbles.

Why it works:

You've probably noticed how water beads up on a window after it rains. That's because water **molecules** pull together. A water bubble doesn't last long because the water pulls in tight, squeezing out the air. Soap molecules are different. One end of a soap molecule is attracted to water, but the other end pushes water away. The soap loosens the water's pull just enough to let it hold air. But the mixture is still strong enough to hold the bubble together as it floats along.

molecule—the atoms making up the smallest unit of a substance

DOUBLE BUBBLES

One bubble is great. Two bubbles are better. Blow a bubble inside a bubble and watch them both grow. This activity is tricky. Keep trying until you can do it!

What you need:

- two straws
- bubble juice (see page 8)

What you do:

straw A

straw B

1 Wet the sides of straw A with bubble juice.

2 Dip the end of straw B into the juice and blow a bubble. Keep it on the end of straw B.

Make sure to keep your straws moist. If bubbles touch a dry straw, they'll pop.

straw B

straw A

straw A to the bubble on straw B. Use straw A
to slowly pull the bubble away from straw B.
Your bubble should be
hanging from straw A.

straw A

straw B

straw B

straw A

4 Dip straw B into the
bubble juice again, and
slide it inside the bubble.

5 Slowly blow a second bubble inside the first. As the
inside bubble grows, the outside bubble will too.

Why it works:

Bubbles are round because the air inside pushes in all directions
against the liquid skin. As you blow, the air causes the bubble to **expand**.
When you blow the second bubble, the air gets trapped between the
skins of the two bubbles. As the inside bubble grows, the trapped air
pushes even harder against the outside bubble. The added pressure
makes the outside bubble expand too.

expand—to increase in size

FiZZLe OUT

Save your breath. You don't have to blow out this candle. Let an invisible gas do the job for you. Grab an adult to light the flame. Then sit back and let the gas bubbles go to work.

What you need:

- bubble gum
- birthday candle
- mug
- 1 tablespoon (15 mL) baking soda
- matches
- 1 tablespoon (15 mL) lemon juice

If you don't have lemon juice, you can use vinegar instead.

1 Chew up a piece of bubble gum. Use it to stand a candle up in the center of a mug.

2 Spread baking soda around the candle.

3 Have an adult use matches to light the candle.

4 Pour lemon juice into the mug. Be careful not to pour it on the candle flame. Watch as the flame fizzles out.

Why it works:

Fire needs **oxygen** to burn. The lemon juice and baking soda react to make carbon dioxide. As the new gas fills the mug, it pushes out the oxygen. When the oxygen is all gone, the candle goes out. Poof!

oxygen—a colorless, odorless gas found naturally in the air

Personal Puffer

Here's a lazy way to blow bubbles. First use a simple chemical reaction to make a gas. Then put that gas to work blowing bubbles out of a bottle.

What you need:

- 1 cup (240 mL) water
- empty drink bottle
- fizzing antacid tablet
- bubble juice (see page 8)

What you do:

1 Pour water into the bottle.

2 Break the antacid tablet in half. Drop both pieces into the bottle.

14

3 Use your finger to rub bubble juice over the opening of the bottle. You should see a thin film covering the opening before the bubble forms and floats away.

If you don't have any fizzing antacid tablets, don't worry. Use ¼ cup (60 mL) vinegar and 1 teaspoon (5 mL) of baking soda instead.

4 Keep adding bubble juice to the opening of the bottle until it stops "blowing" bubbles.

Why it works:

In the experiment "Sizzling Soda" on page 6, you found out that baking soda makes carbon dioxide when it mixes with an acid. A fizzing antacid tablet is made of baking soda and citric acid. When the tablet hits the water, the chemical reaction starts. The carbon dioxide bubbles rise to the surface and push air out of the bottle. Because bubble juice covers the bottle opening, the juice surrounds the air, and the bubble floats away.

Bobbing Blobs

Oil and water don't mix, but bubbles can blend them with some amazing results. Kick back and watch as blobs of liquid bob and float like magic.

What you need:

- clear jar or bottle
- water
- food coloring
- spoon
- baby oil
- fizzing antacid tablet

Don't put the cap on the jar or the bubbles won't last as long.

1 Fill the jar about ¼ full of water.

2 Add a few drops of food coloring. Use a spoon to stir the coloring into the water.

3 Pour baby oil into the jar, leaving about 1 inch (2.5 cm) of room at the top.

4 Break the antacid tablet in half. Drop both pieces into the jar. Sit back and watch as the colored bubbles rise to the top.

Why it works:

When you add the oil to the bottle, you'll notice that it floats on top of the water. Oil is less **dense** than water. Just like in "Personal Puffer" on page 14, the antacid makes bubbles of carbon dioxide gas. As the bubbles rise, they drag blobs of colored water with them. When the bubbles reach the surface, they pop. Then the water sinks back to the bottom.

dense—crowded or thick; the density of an object or liquid is how heavy or light it is for its size

Foaming Fountain

Hydrogen peroxide isn't just for cleaning cuts. You can use it to make a sudsy fountain of foam. Be sure to set this up in the kitchen sink so you can wash the sticky remains away.

What you need:

- 2 tablespoons (30 mL) warm water
- bowl
- 1 teaspoon (5 mL) live active yeast
- spoon
- empty drink bottle
- funnel
- 1¼ cups (300 mL) hydrogen peroxide
- 1 tablespoon (15 mL) dish soap

What you do:

1 Pour water into a bowl. Add yeast and stir gently.

For an even foamier experience, you can get a stronger dose of hydrogen peroxide at a beauty supply store. Look for the label "20-volume hydrogen peroxide."

2 Set the bottle in the sink. Stick a funnel in the bottle.

18

3 Pour hydrogen peroxide through the funnel into the bottle.

4 Add the dish soap to the bottle.

5 Pour the yeast mixture into the bottle and pull out the funnel.

Why it works:

Hydrogen peroxide breaks down into water and oxygen. It takes a long time for hydrogen peroxide to break down on its own. But yeast has a chemical that speeds things up. The hydrogen peroxide breaks down quickly, and oxygen gas bubbles out. The bubbles stir up the soap to create a moving pile of suds.

not Quite the Midas Touch

Someone with the Midas touch is supposed to be able to turn anything into gold. You can't pull that off, but you can use a chemical reaction to make old silver shine again.

What you need:

- non-aluminum saucepan
- aluminum foil
- tarnished silver, such as silverware or earrings that have turned gray or black
- bowl
- 4 cups (960 mL) water
- 1 tablespoon (15 mL) baking soda
- 1 teaspoon (5 mL) salt

It may take more than 30 minutes to clean silver that has a lot of black tarnish.

1 Line the saucepan with aluminum foil with the shiny side facing up.

2 Lay pieces of tarnished silver on the aluminum foil. Arrange the pieces so the silver touches as much of the aluminum foil as possible.

3 In a bowl, mix water, baking soda, and salt.

4 Pour the mixture into the saucepan. Have an adult heat the mixture until it boils.

5 Turn down the heat and let the water simmer until the tarnish is gone. Allow the water to cool before you remove the silver.

Why it works:

Silver turns gray and black because it has a chemical reaction with **sulfur** in the air. Boiling the water with baking soda separates the sulfur from the silver. You may have noticed that as the silver cleans up, the aluminum foil turns gray. Aluminum reacts with sulfur more strongly than silver does. Once the sulfur is freed from the silver, it joins up with the aluminum foil.

sulfur—a chemical element used in gunpowder, matches, and fertilizer

Fire Away!

Grab some things from your kitchen pantry. Then head outside for a little science shooting practice. Fire a cork out of a bottle using just the power of vinegar and baking soda. Just make sure the cork is pointed away from people, animals, and windows!

What you need:

- 1¼ cups (300 mL) vinegar
- empty drink bottle
- ½ tablespoon (7.5 mL) baking soda
- toilet paper
- safety goggles
- cork that fits tightly in the mouth of the bottle

What if the cork doesn't fit tightly into the bottle? No problem. Just wrap a few layers of duct tape around the cork to make it bigger.

What you do:

1 Measure vinegar. Pour the vinegar into an empty bottle.

2 Dump baking soda onto a square of toilet paper.

3 Roll up the piece of toilet paper into a tube. Twist the ends so that the tube holds the baking soda.

4 Put on safety goggles. Grab your supplies and head outside.

5 Drop the bundle of baking soda into the bottle. Quickly jam the cork into the bottle.

6 Point the bottle toward the sky and hang on.

Why it works:

Vinegar is a weak acid. Just like you saw in "Sizzling Soda," when you mix baking soda and an acid you start a chemical reaction that makes carbon dioxide gas. The gas collects until the bottle is full. When there's nowhere else to go, the gas forces the cork out of the bottle. Pow!

INFLATION STATION

Can creatures smaller than a needle point blow up a balloon? They can if they work together! Feed a little sugar to some yeast and watch these tiny creatures in action.

What you need:

- balloon
- funnel
- 1 packet live active yeast
- empty drink bottle with lid
- 2 tablespoons (30 mL) sugar
- 1 cup (240 mL) of warm water

What you do:

1 Stretch a balloon several times to loosen it up.

Yeast work quickly in warm water, but will die in water that's too hot. Use water that is just a little warmer than your fingers.

2 Use a funnel to pour one packet of yeast into a plastic bottle.

3 Add sugar and water to the bottle.

4 Put the lid on the bottle and shake it until everything is mixed.

5 Remove the lid and stretch the balloon over the top of the bottle.

6 Check on the balloon in one hour. The yeast mixture will bubble and the balloon will slowly fill up.

Why it works:

When you opened the packet of yeast, you might have noticed that the yeast looks like tiny beads. Each tiny ball of yeast contains millions of **microorganisms**. As the tiny creatures eat the sugar, they make carbon dioxide gas. The gas bubbles up to the top of the bottle and fills the balloon.

microorganism—a living thing too small to be seen without a microscope

SODA SHOOTER

Drive the carbon dioxide out of soda and send your soft drink soaring. This experiment only starts in the kitchen. If it ends there, you'll have a huge mess to clean.

What you need:

- bottle of soda
- modeling clay
- straw
- 1 tablespoon (15 mL) of rock or kosher salt
- small paper cup
- safety goggles

If you can't take this project outside, try it in a shower for easy cleanup.

1 Drink or pour out about one-fourth of the soda.

2 Break off a chunk of modeling clay that's a little bigger than the mouth of the bottle. Wrap the clay around the middle of the straw.

3 Set the straw in the bottle. Shape the clay over the mouth of the bottle to make a seal around the straw.

SODA SHOOTER continues on next page ⟶

4 Pour the salt into a small paper cup. Then put on your safety goggles and head outside.

5 Tilt the straw and the modeling clay to the side.

6 The next two steps need to be done very fast. Dump the salt into the bottle all at once.

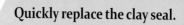

7 Quickly replace the clay seal.

8 Hold the bottle away from you and watch the soda shoot!

Why it works:

Soda is fizzy because it is filled with tiny bubbles of carbon dioxide gas. These tiny bubbles gather along the rough edges of the salt and join to make bigger bubbles. The big bubbles are too large to stay put, so they come rushing out of the soda. The gas molecules spread out and raise the **pressure** in the bottle. Something has to give, so the soda takes the only way out—through the straw.

pressure—a force that pushes on something

GLOSSARY

acid (AS-id)—a substance with a sour taste that reacts easily with other substances

carbon dioxide (KAHR-buhn dy-AHK-syd)—a colorless, odorless gas made of oxygen and carbon

chemical reaction (KEM-i-kuhl ree-AK-shuhn)—a process in which one substance changes into another

dense (DENSS)—crowded or thick; the density of an object or liquid is how heavy or light it is for its size

expand (ek-SPAND)—to increase in size

gas (GASS)—a substance that spreads to fill any space that holds it

microorganism (mye-kroh-OR-guh-niz-uhm)—a living thing too small to be seen without a microscope

molecule (MOL-uh-kyool)—the atoms making up the smallest unit of a substance

oxygen (OK-suh-juhn)—a colorless, odorless gas found naturally in the air

pressure (PRESH-ur)—a force that pushes on something

sulfur (SUHL-fur)—a chemical element used in gunpowder, matches, and fertilizer

Read More

Cobb, Vicki, and Kathy Darling. *We Dare You!: Hundreds of Fun Science Bets, Challenges, and Experiments You Can Do at Home.* New York: Skyhorse Publishing, 2008.

O'Neal, Claire. *A Project Guide to Volcanoes.* Earth Science Projects for Kids. Hockessin, Del.: Mitchell Lane Publishers, 2011.

Winston, Robert. *Science Rocks!: Unleash the Mad Scientist in You!* New York: Dorling Kindersley Publishing, 2011.

Internet Sites

FactHound offers a safe, fun way to find Internet sites related to this book. All of the sites on FactHound have been researched by our staff.

Here's all you do:

Visit *www.facthound.com*

Type in this code: **9781429654258**

Index

acids, 7, 15, 23

baking soda, 6, 7, 12–13, 15,
    20–21, 22–23
Bobbing Blobs, 16–17
Bubble Juice, 8–9

carbon dioxide, 7, 13, 15, 17,
    23, 25, 26, 29
chemical reactions, 5, 14,
    15, 20, 21, 23

density, 17
Double Bubbles, 10–11

fire, 12, 13
Fire Away!, 22–23
fizzing antacid tablets,
    14–15, 16–17
Fizzle Out, 12–13
Foaming Fountain, 18–19

hydrogen peroxide, 18–19

Inflation Station, 24–25

lemon juice, 12–13

molecules, 9, 29

Not Quite the Midas
    Touch, 20–21

oil, 16–17
orange juice, 6, 7
oxygen, 13, 19

Personal Puffer, 14-15, 17
pressure, 11, 29

salt, 20–21, 26–29
silver, 20–21
Sizzling Soda, 6–7, 15, 23
soap, 8–9, 18–19
Soda Shooter, 26–29
sugar, 24–25
sulfur, 21

vinegar, 12, 15, 22–23

water, 4, 8–9, 14–15, 16–17,
    18–19, 20–21, 24–25

yeast, 18–19, 24–25